INSPIRATIONS

Also by Julia Cameron

NONFICTION

The Artist's Way *(with Mark Bryan)*
The Artist's Way Morning Pages Journal
The Artist's Date Book
(illustrated by Elizabeth Cameron)
The Vein of Gold
The Right to Write
God Is No Laughing Matter
Supplies *(illustrated by Elizabeth Cameron)*
God Is Dog Spelled Backwards
(illustrated by Elizabeth Cameron)
Heartsteps
Blessings
Transitions
The Artist's Way at Work *(with Mark Bryan
and Catherine Allen)*
Money Drunk, Money Sober *(with Mark Bryan)*

FICTION

The Dark Room
Popcorn: Hollywood Stories

INSPIRATIONS

Meditations from The Artist's Way

JULIA CAMERON

JEREMY P. TARCHER/PUTNAM

a member of Penguin Putnam Inc.

New York

Most Tarcher/Putnam books are available at special quantity discounts for bulk purchase for sales promotions, premiums, fund-raising, and educational needs. Special books or book excerpts also can be created to fit specific needs. For details, write Putnam Special Markets, 375 Hudson Street, New York, NY 10014.

Jeremy P. Tarcher/Putnam
a member of
Penguin Putnam Inc.
375 Hudson Street
New York, NY 10014
www.penguinputnam.com

Library of Congress Cataloging-in-Publication Data

Cameron, Julia.
Inspirations : meditations from The artist's way / by Julia Cameron.
p.   cm.
ISBN 1-58542-102-2
1. Creative ability—Quotations, maxims, etc.   2. Self-actualization
(Psychology)—Quotations, maxims, etc.   3. Creation (Literary,
artistic, etc.)—Quotations, maxims, etc.   I. Cameron, Julia.
Artist's way.   II. Title.
BF408.C1755   2001   2001018893
153.3'5—dc21

Printed in the United States of America

1   3   5   7   9   10   8   6   4   2

This book is printed on acid-free paper. ∞

Book design by Claire Vaccaro and Jennifer Ann Daddio

INVOCATION

Art is an act of the soul, not the intellect. When we are dealing with people's dreams—their visions, really—we are in the realm of the sacred. We are involved with forces and energies larger than our own. We invoke the Great Creator when we invoke our own creativity, and that creative force has the power to alter lives, fulfill destinies, and answer our dreams.

All of us are creative. Just as blood is a fact of your physical body and nothing you invented, creativity is a fact of your spiritual body and nothing that you must invent.

Creativity is the natural order of life. Life is energy: pure creative energy. There is an underlying, in-dwelling creative force infusing all of life—including ourselves. When we open ourselves to our creativity, we open ourselves to the Creator's creativity within us and our lives.

We are, ourselves, creations. We, in turn, are meant to continue creativity by being creative ourselves. Creativity is God's gift to us. Using our creativity is our gift back to God. The refusal to be creative is self-will and is counter to our true nature.

When we open ourselves to exploring our creativity, we open ourselves to God: good orderly direction. As we open our creative channel to the Creator, many gentle but powerful changes are to be expected.

It is safe to open ourselves up to greater and greater creativity. Our creative dreams and yearnings come from a divine source. As we move toward our dreams, we move toward our divinity.

In order to retrieve your creativity, you need to find it. You do this by an apparently pointless process I call the Morning Pages. *The Morning Pages are the primary tool of creative recovery.* What are Morning Pages? Put simply, the Morning Pages are three pages of longhand morning writing, strictly stream-of-consciousness.

There is no wrong way to do Morning Pages. These daily morning meanderings are not meant to be *art.* Although occasionally colorful, the Morning Pages are often negative, frequently fragmented, often self-pitying, repetitive, stilted or babyish, angry or bland—even silly sounding. Good! All that angry, whiny, petty stuff that you write down in the morning stands between you and your creativity.

Over any considerable period of time, the Morning Pages perform spiritual chiropractic. They realign our values. If we are to the left or the right of our personal truth, the pages will point out the need for a course adjustment. We will become aware of our drift and correct it—if only to hush the pages up. Just as an athlete accustomed to running becomes irritable when he is unable to get his miles in, so, too, those of us now accustomed to Morning Pages will notice an irritability when we let them slide. We are tempted, always, to reverse cause and effect: "I was too crabby to write them," instead of "I didn't write them so I am crabby."

As artists, we must learn to be self-nourishing. We must become alert enough to consciously replenish our creative resources as we draw on them—to restock the trout pond, so to speak. I call this process *filling the well*. In filling the well, think magic. Think delight. Think fun. Do not think duty. Do not do what you *should* do—spiritual sit-ups like reading a dull but recommended critical text. Do what intrigues you, explore what interests you; think mystery, not mastery.

You need artist dates. Your artist needs to be taken out, pampered, and listened to. But what exactly *is* an artist date? An artist date is a block of time, perhaps two hours weekly, especially set aside and committed to nurturing your creative consciousness, your inner artist. In its most primary form, the artist date is an excursion, a solo play date that you preplan and defend against all interlopers.

Art is an image-using system. In order to create, we draw from our inner well. This inner well, an artistic reservoir, is ideally like a well-stocked trout pond. Any extended period or piece of work draws heavily on our artistic well. Over-tapping the well, like overfishing the pond, leaves us with diminished resources. We fish in vain for the images we require. Our work dries up and we wonder why, "just when it was going so well." The truth is that work can dry up *because* it is going so well. This is why we must remember to fill the well. Serious work demands serious play. This is why it is called the play of ideas.

Trusting our creativity is new behavior for many of us. It may feel quite threatening initially, not only to us but also to our intimates. We may feel—and look—erratic. This erraticism is a normal part of getting unstuck, pulling free from the muck that has blocked us. It is important to remember that at first flush, going *sane* feels just like going crazy. Growth is an erratic forward movement: two steps forward, one step back. Remember that and be very gentle with yourself. A creative recovery is a healing process.

The process of identifying a *self* inevitably involves loss as well as gain. We discover our boundaries, and those boundaries by definition separate us from our fellows. As we clarify our perceptions, we lose our misconceptions. As we eliminate ambiguity, we lose illusion as well. We arrive at clarity, and clarity creates change. Some of our friends may feel threatened. If they do, they may try to sabotage our healthy changes.

M any blocked people are actually very powerful and creative personalities who have been made to feel guilty about their own strengths and gifts. Without being acknowledged, they are often used as batteries by their families and friends, who feel free to both use their creative energies and disparage them. Often, creativity is blocked by our falling in with other people's plans for us. We want to set aside time for our creative work, but we feel we *should* do something else instead. As blocked creatives, we focus not on our responsibilities to ourselves, but on our responsibilities to others. We tend to think such behavior makes us good people. It doesn't. It makes us frustrated people.

Often we involve ourselves with crazymakers in order to avoid being creative ourselves. Crazymakers are those personalities that create storm centers. They are often charismatic, frequently charming, highly inventive, and powerfully persuasive. And, for the creative person in their vicinity, they are enormously destructive. If you are involved with a crazymaker, it is very important that you admit this fact. Admit that you are being used—and admit that you are using them to sabotage your own trajectory. As much as you are being exploited by your crazymaker, you, too, are using that person to block your creative flow.

Do not expect your crazymaker friends to applaud your recovery. That's like expecting your best friends from the bar to celebrate your sobriety. How can they when their own drinking is something they want to hold on to?

M ost of the time when we are blocked in an area of our life, it is because we feel safer that way. We may not be happy, but at least we know what we are—unhappy. Much fear of our own creativity is the fear of the unknown. If I am fully creative, what will it mean? What will happen to me and to others? We have some pretty awful notions about what *could* happen. So, rather than find out, we decide to stay blocked. This is seldom a conscious decision. It is more often an unconscious response to internalized negative beliefs. We may believe artists are crazy. If so, we become shadow artists.

Too intimidated to become artists themselves, very often too low in self-worth to even recognize that they have an artistic dream, many people become shadow artists instead. Artists themselves, but ignorant of their true identity, shadow artists are to be found shadowing declared artists. Unable to recognize that they themselves may possess the creativity they so admire, they often date or marry people who actively pursue the art career that they themselves secretly long for.

Artists love other artists. Shadow artists are gravitating to their rightful tribe but cannot yet claim their birthright. Very often audacity, not talent, makes one person an artist and another a shadow artist—hiding in the shadows, afraid to step out and expose the dream to the light, fearful that it will disintegrate to the touch. Shadow artists often choose shadow careers—those close to the desired art, even parallel to it, but not the art itself.

As blocked creatives, we often sit on the side lines critiquing those in the game. "He's not so talented," we may say of a currently hot artist. And we may be right about that. All too often, it is bravado and not talent that moves an artist to center stage. As blocked creatives, we tend to regard these bogus spotlight grabbers with animosity. We need to focus on *our* creativity, not their lack of it.

Most blocked creatives carry unacknowledged either/or reasoning that stands between them and their work. To become unblocked we must recognize our either/or thinking. "I can either be romantically happy *or* an artist." "I can either be financially successful *or* an artist." It is possible, quite possible, to be both an artist and romantically fulfilled. It is quite possible to be an artist and financially successful. Negative beliefs are exactly that: beliefs, not facts. The world was never flat, although everyone believed it was. You are not dumb, crazy, egomaniacal, grandiose, or silly just because you falsely believe yourself to be.

As your recovery progresses, you will come to experience a more comfortable faith in your creator and your creator within. You will learn that it is actually easier to write than not write, paint than not paint, and so forth. You will learn to enjoy the process of being a creative channel and to surrender your need to control the result. You will discover the joy of practicing your creativity. The process, not the product, will become your focus.

If you think of the universe as a vast electrical sea in which you are immersed and from which you are formed, opening to your creativity changes you from something bobbing in that sea to a more fully functioning, more conscious, more cooperative part of that ecosystem.

The heart of creativity is an experience of the mystical union; the heart of the mystical union is an experience of creativity. Those who speak in spiritual terms routinely refer to God as the Creator but seldom see *creator* as the literal term for *artist*. You are seeking to forge a creative alliance, artist-to-artist with the Great Creator. Accepting this concept can greatly expand your creative possibilities.

Being blocked had its "payoffs." We could wonder and worry about our arrogance instead of being humble enough to ask for help to move through our fear. We could fantasize about art instead of doing the work. By not asking the Great Creator's help with our creativity, and by not seeing the Great Creator's hand in our creativity, we could proceed to righteously ignore our creativity and never have to take the risks of fulfilling it.

There is a recognizable ebb and flow to the process of recovering our creative selves. As we gain strength, so will some of the attacks of self-doubt. This is normal, and we can deal with these stronger attacks when we see them as symptoms of recovery. As you learn to recognize, nurture, and protect your inner artist, you will be able to move beyond pain and creative constriction. You will learn ways to recognize and resolve fear, remove emotional scar tissue, and strengthen your confidence. Damaging old ideas about creativity will be explored and discarded.

Creativity is an experience, a spiritual experience. It does not matter which way you think of it: creativity leading to spirituality or spirituality leading to creativity. In fact, I do not make a distinction between the two. Setting skepticism aside, even briefly, can make for very interesting explorations. In creative recovery, it is not necessary that we change any of our beliefs. It is necessary that we examine them. More than anything else, creative recovery is an exercise in open-mindedness. Picture your mind as a room with the door slightly ajar. Nudging that door open a bit more is what makes for open-mindedness.

People frequently believe the creative life is grounded in fantasy. The more difficult truth is that creativity is grounded in reality, in the particular, the focused, the well observed, or the specifically imagined. Very often, a creative block manifests itself as an addiction to fantasy or even to "worry." Rather than working or living in the now, we spin our wheels and indulge in daydreams of could have, would have, should have. One of the great misconceptions about the artistic life is that it entails great swathes of aimlessness. The truth is that a creative life involves great swathes of attention.

Attention is a way to connect and survive. The reward for attention is always healing. It may begin as the healing of a particular pain— the lost lover, the sickly child, the shattered dream. But what is healed, finally, is the pain that underlies all pain: the pain that we all feel, as Rilke phrases it, "unutterably alone." More than anything else, attention is an act of connection.

Our focused attention is critical to filling the well. We need to encounter our life experiences, not ignore them. Many of us read compulsively to screen our awareness. On a crowded (interesting) train, we train our attention on a newspaper, losing sights and sounds around us— all images for the well. Remember that the more you feel yourself to be terra incognita, the more certain you can be that the recovery process is working. You are your own promised land, your own new frontier.

As we lose our vagueness about ourself, our values, our life situation, we become available to the moment. It is there, in the particular, that we contact the creative self. Art lies in the moment of encounter: we meet our truth and we meet ourselves; we meet ourselves and we meet our self-expression. We become original because we become something specific: an origin from which work flows.

As we seek to become more creative, we are led by the Great Creator. The Morning Pages symbolize our willingness to speak to and hear God. They lead us into many other changes that also come from God and lead us to God. This is the hand of God moving through your hand as you write. It is very powerful. It is difficult for us to realize that this process of going inside and writing Morning Pages can open an inner door through which our creator helps and guides us. Our willingness swings this inner door open.

Creativity is a spiritual issue. Any progress is made by leaps of faith, some small and some large. God as my source is a simple but completely effective plan for living. It removes negative dependency—and anxiety—from our lives by assuring us that God will provide. Our job is to listen for how.

Dependence on the creator within is really freedom from all other dependencies. Paradoxically, it is also the only route to real intimacy with other human beings. Freed from our terrible fears of abandonment, we are able to live with more spontaneity. Freed from our constant demands for more and more reassurance, our fellows are able to love us back without feeling so burdened.

Remembering that God is our source, we are in the spiritual position of having an unlimited bank account. Most of us never consider how powerful the Creator really is. Instead, we draw very limited amounts of the power available to us. We decide how powerful God is for us. We unconsciously set a limit on how much God can give us or help us. We are stingy with ourselves.

One of the chief barriers to accepting God's generosity is our limited notion of what we are in fact able to accomplish. We may tune in to the voice of the creator within, hear a message, and then discount it as crazy or impossible— "too big." On the one hand, we take ourselves very seriously and don't want to look like idiots pursuing some patently grandiose scheme. On the other hand, we don't take ourselves—or God—seriously enough, and so we define as grandiose many schemes that, with God's help, may fall well within our grasp.

Many of us have made a virtue out of deprivation. We have embraced a long-suffering artistic anorexia as a martyr's cross. We have used it to feed a false sense of spirituality grounded in being good, meaning *superior*. This seductive, faux spirituality is the Virtue Trap. Spirituality has often been misused as a route to an unloving solitude, a stance where we proclaim ourselves above our human nature. This spiritual superiority is really only one more form of denial.

Afraid to appear selfish, we lose our self. We become self-destructive. Because this self-murder is something we seek passively rather than consciously act out, we are often blind to its poisonous grip on us. Virtuous to a fault, trapped creatives have destroyed the true self, the self that didn't meet with much approval as a child, the self who heard repeatedly, "Don't be selfish!" The true self is a disturbing character, healthy and occasionally anarchistic, who knows how to play, how to say "no" to others and "yes" to itself.

The question "Are you self-destructive?" is asked so frequently that we seldom hear it accurately. What it means is *Are you destructive of your self?* And what that really asks us is *Are you destructive of your true nature?*

One reason we are miserly with ourselves is scarcity thinking. We don't want our luck to run out. We don't want to overspend our spiritual abundance. Again, we are limiting our flow by anthropomorphizing God into a capricious parent figure. Remembering that God is our source, an energy flow that *likes* to extend itself, we become more able to tap our creative power effectively.

For many of us, raised to believe that money is the real source of security, a dependence on God feels foolhardy, suicidal, even laughable. When we consider the lilies of the fields, we think they are quaint, too out of it for the modern world. Listening to the siren song of *more*, we are deaf to the still small voice waiting in our soul to whisper, "You're enough."

In recovering from our creative blocks, it is necessary to go gently and slowly. What we are after here is the healing of old wounds—not the creation of new ones. No high jumping, please! Mistakes are necessary! Stumbles are normal. These are baby steps. Progress, not perfection, is what we should be asking of ourselves. Too far, too fast, and we can undo ourselves. Creative recovery is like marathon training. We want to log ten slow miles for every one fast mile.

An artist must have downtime, time to do nothing. Defending our right to such time takes courage, conviction, and resiliency. Such time, space, and quiet will strike our family and friends as withdrawal from them. It is. For an artist, withdrawal is necessary. Without it, the artist in us feels vexed, angry, out of sorts. If such deprivation continues, our artist becomes sullen, depressed, hostile. We eventually become like cornered animals, snarling at our family and friends to leave us alone and stop making unreasonable demands. Often, they *are* making unreasonable demands.

Creative living requires the luxury of time, which we carve out for ourselves—even if it's fifteen minutes for quick Morning Pages and a ten-minute minibath after work. Creative living requires the luxury of space for ourselves, even if all we manage to carve out is one special bookshelf and a windowsill that is ours. (My study has a window shelf of paperweights and seashells.) Remember that your artist is a youngster and youngsters like things that are "mine." My chair. My book. My pillow. Even my fifteen minutes.

For those of us who have become artistically anorectic—yearning to be creative and refusing to feed that hunger in ourselves so that we become more and more focused on our deprivation—a little authentic luxury can go a long way. The key word here is *authentic*. Because art is born in expansion, in a belief in sufficient supply, it is critical that we pamper ourselves for the sense of abundance it brings to us. A box of raspberries or a small bouquet can bring a big shift in optimism.

All too often, we become blocked and blame it on our lack of money. This is *never* an authentic block. The actual block is our feeling of constriction, our sense of powerlessness. Art requires us to empower ourselves with choice. At the most basic level, this means choosing to do self-care.

Many of us equate difficulty with virtue—and art with fooling around. Hard work is good. A terrible job must be building our moral fiber. Something—a talent for painting, say—that comes to us easily and seems compatible with us must be some sort of cheap trick, not to be taken seriously. Creativity lives in paradox: serious art is born from serious play.

On the one hand, we give lip service to the notion that God wants us to be happy, joyous, and free. On the other, we secretly think that God wants us to be broke if we are going to be so decadent as to want to be artists. Do we have any proof at all for these ideas about God? We are operating out of the toxic old idea that God's will for us and our will for us are at opposite ends of the table. "I want to be an actress, but God wants me to wait tables in hash joints," the scenario goes. "So if I try to be an actress, I will end up slinging hash." Maybe we won't. The universe falls in with worthy plans and most especially with festive and expansive ones.

All too often, when people talk about creative work, they emphasize strategy. Neophytes are advised of the Machiavellian devices they must employ to break into the field. I think this is a lot of rubbish. If you ask an artist how he got where he is, he will not describe breaking in but instead will talk of a series of lucky breaks. Joseph Campbell calls these breaks "a thousand unseen helping hands." I call them synchronicity. It is my contention that you can count on them.

Looking at God's creation, it is pretty clear that the Creator itself did not know when to stop. There is not one pink flower, or even fifty pink flowers, but hundreds. Snowflakes, of course, are the ultimate exercise in sheer creative glee. No two alike. This Creator looks suspiciously like someone who just might send us support for our creative ventures.

Life is what we make of it. Whether we conceive of an inner god force or another, outer God, doesn't matter. Relying on that force does. "Ask and you shall receive. Knock and it shall be opened to you . . ." These words are among the more challenging ones ascribed to Jesus Christ. They suggest the possibility of scientific method: ask (experiment) and see what happens (record the results). This can be done with our art.

In order to thrive as artists—and, one could argue, as people—we need to be available to the universal flow. When we put a stopper on our capacity for joy by anorectically declining the small gifts of life, we turn aside the larger gifts as well.

For many blocked creatives, it takes a little work to even *imagine* ourselves having luxury. Luxury is a learned practice for most of us. Blocked creatives are often the Cinderellas of the world. Focused on others at the expense of ourselves, we may even be threatened by the idea of spoiling ourselves for once.

What we are talking about when we discuss luxury is very often a shift in consciousness more than flow—although as we acknowledge and invite what feels luxurious to us, we may indeed trigger an increased flow. Most of us harbor a secret belief that work has to be work and not play, and that anything we really want to do—like write, act, dance—must be considered frivolous and be placed a distant second. This is not true.

Turn aside your dream and it will come back to you again. Get willing to follow it again and a second mysterious door will swing open. The universe is prodigal in its support. We are often miserly in what we accept. What we really want to do is what we are really meant to do. When we do what we are meant to do, money comes to us, doors open for us, we feel useful, and the work we do feels like play to us.

When we have engaged the creator within to heal us, many changes and shifts in our attitudes begin to occur. Many of these will not be recognizable at first as healing. In fact, they may seem crazy and even destructive. At best, they will seem eccentric. There will be a change in energy patterns. Your dreams will become stronger and clearer, both by night and by day. You will find yourself remembering your nighttime dreams, and by day, daydreams will catch your attention. Fantasy, of a benign and unexpected sort, will begin to crop up. Shifts in taste and perception frequently accompany shifts in identity. One of the clearest signals that something healthy is afoot is the impulse to weed out, sort through, and discard old clothes, papers, and belongings.

Faced with impending change, change we have set in motion through our own hand, we want to mutiny, curl up in a ball, bawl our eyes out. "No pain, no gain," the nasty slogan has it. And we resent this pain no matter what gain it is bringing us. It makes us angry. In the recovery of a blocked artist, anger is a sign of health. Anger is the firestorm that signals the death of our old life. Anger is the fuel that propels us into our new one. Anger is not a tool, not a master. Anger is meant to be tapped into and drawn upon. Used properly, anger is *use-full*.

Sloth, apathy, and despair are the enemy. Anger is not. Anger is our friend. Not a nice friend. Not a gentle friend. But a very, very loyal friend. It will always tell us when we have betrayed ourselves. It will always tell us that it is time to act in our own best interest.

Anger is meant to be listened to. Anger is a voice, a shout, a plea, a demand. Anger is meant to be respected. Why? Because anger is a *map*. Anger shows us what our boundaries are. Anger shows us where we want to go. It lets us see where we've been and lets us know when we haven't liked it. Anger points the way, not just the finger.

Anger is meant to be acted upon. It is not meant to be acted out. Anger points the direction. We are meant to use anger as fuel to take the actions we need to move where our anger points us. With a little thought, we can usually translate the message that our anger is sending us.

Working with Morning Pages, you may well be experiencing a sense of both bafflement and faith. You are no longer stuck, but you cannot tell where you are going. You may feel that this can't keep up. You may long for the time when there was no sense of possibility, when you felt more victimized, when you didn't realize how many small things you could do to improve your own life.

We've all heard that the unexamined life is not worth living, but consider too that the unlived life is not worth examining. The success of a creative recovery hinges on our ability to move out of the head and into action. This brings us squarely to risk. Most of us are practiced at talking ourselves out of risk. We are skilled speculators on the probable pain of self-exposure. This means we avoid risk.

All too often, when people look to having a more creative life, they hold an unspoken and often unacknowledged expectation, or fear, that they will be abandoning life as they know it. Blocked creatives like to think they are looking at changing their whole life in one fell swoop. This form of grandiosity is very often its own undoing. By setting the jumps too high and making the price tag too great, the recovering artist sets defeat in motion.

Creative people are dramatic, and we use negative drama to scare ourselves out of our creativity with this notion of wholesale and often destructive change. Fantasizing about pursuing our art full-time, we fail to pursue it part-time— or at all. Rather than take a scary baby step toward our dreams, we rush to the edge of the cliff and then stand there, quaking, saying, "I can't leap. I can't. I can't . . ."

Most blocked creatives have an active addiction to anxiety. We prefer the low-grade pain and occasional heart-stopping panic attack to the drudgery of small and simple daily steps in the right direction. Indulging ourselves in a frantic fantasy of what our life would look like if we were real artists, we fail to see the many small creative changes that we could make at this very moment. Filling the form means that we must work with what we have rather than languish in complaints over what we have not.

Take one small daily action instead of indulging in the big questions. When we allow ourselves to wallow in the big questions, we fail to find the small answers. What we are talking about here is a concept of change grounded in respect—respect for where we are as well as where we wish to go. We are looking not to grand strokes of change—although they may come—but instead to the act of creatively husbanding all that is in the present: this job, this house, this relationship.

One of the most important tasks in artistic recovery is learning to call things—and ourselves—by the right names. Most of us have spent years using the wrong names for our behaviors. We have wanted to create and we have been unable to create and we have called that inability *laziness.*

Being blocked and being lazy are two different things. The blocked artist typically expends a great deal of energy—just not visibly. The blocked artist spends energy on self-hatred, on regret, on grief, and on jealousy. The blocked artist spends energy on self-doubt.

Finding it hard to begin a project does not mean you will not be able to do it. It means you will need help—from your higher power, from supportive friends, and from yourself. First of all, you must give yourself permission to begin small and go in baby steps. These steps must be rewarded. Setting impossible goals creates enormous fear, which creates procrastination, which we wrongly call laziness. *Do not call procrastination laziness. Call it fear.*

Being an artist requires enthusiasm more than discipline. Enthusiasm is not an emotional state. It is a spiritual commitment, a loving surrender to our creative process, a loving recognition of all the creativity around us. Enthusiasm (from the Greek, "filled with God") is an ongoing energy supply tapped into the flow of life itself. Enthusiasm is grounded in play, not work. Far from being a brain-numbed soldier, our artist is actually our child within, our inner playmate. As with all playmates, it is joy, not duty, that makes for a lasting bond.

Remember that art is process. The process is supposed to be fun. For our purposes, "the journey is always the only arrival" may be interpreted to mean that our creative work is actually our creativity itself at play in the field of time. At the heart of this play is the mystery of joy.

Perfectionism is the enemy of art. Tillie Olsen correctly calls it the "knife of the perfectionist attitude in art." You may call it something else. *Getting it right,* you may call it, or *fixing it before I go any further.* You may call it *having standards.* What you should be calling it is *perfectionism.* Perfectionism has nothing to do with getting it right. It has nothing to do with fixing things. It has nothing to do with standards. Perfectionism is a refusal to let yourself move ahead. It is a loop—an obsessive, debilitating closed system that causes you to get stuck in the details of what you are writing or painting or making and to lose sight of the whole.

To the perfectionist, there is always room for improvement. The perfectionist calls this humility. In reality, it is egotism. It is pride that makes us want to write a perfect script, paint a perfect painting, perform a perfect audition monologue. Perfectionism is not a quest for the best. It is a pursuit of the worst in ourselves, the part that tells us that nothing we do will ever be good enough— that we should try again. No. We should not.

Focused on process, our creative life retains a sense of adventure. Focused on product, the same creative life can feel foolish or barren. We inherit the obsession with product and the idea that art produces finished product from our consumer-oriented society. This focus creates a great deal of creative block. We, as working artists, may want to explore a new artistic area, but we don't see where it will get us. We wonder if it will be good for our career. Fixated on the need to have something to show for our labors, we often deny our curiosities. Every time we do this, we are blocked.

As blocked artists, we unrealistically expect and demand immediate success from ourselves and recognition of that success from others. With that as an unspoken demand, a great many things remain outside our sphere of possibility. Once we are willing to accept that anything worth doing might even be worth doing badly, our options widen. "If I didn't have to do it perfectly, I would try . . ."

We deny that in order to do something well we must first be willing to do it badly. Instead, we opt for setting our limits at the point where we feel assured of success. Living within these bounds, we may feel stifled, smothered, despairing, bored. But, yes, we do feel safe. And safety is a very expensive illusion.

Once you accept that it is natural to create, you can begin to accept a second idea—that the Creator will hand you whatever you need for the project. The minute you are willing to accept the help of this collaborator, you will see useful bits of help everywhere in your life. Be alert: there is a second voice, a higher harmonic, adding to and augmenting your inner creative voice. This voice frequently shows itself in synchronicity.

Art is an act of tuning in and dropping down the well. It is as though all the stories, paintings, music, and performances in the world live just under the surface of our normal consciousness. Like an underground river, they flow through us as a stream of ideas that we can tap down into. As artists, we drop down the well into the stream. We hear what's down there and we act on it—more like taking dictation than anything fancy having to do with art.

Art is not about thinking something up. It is about the opposite—getting something down. The directions are important here. If we are trying to *think something up*, we are straining to reach for something that's just beyond our grasp, "up there, in the stratosphere, where art lives on high." When we *get something down*, there is no strain. We're not doing: we're getting. Someone or something else is doing the doing. Instead of reaching for inventions, we are engaged in listening.

We can learn not only to listen but also to hear with increasing accuracy that inspired, intuitive voice that says, "Do this, try this, say this . . ." If paintings and sculptures wait for us, then sonatas wait for us; books, plays, and poems wait for us too. Our job is simply to get them down. To do that, we drop down the well.

If you feel stuck in your life or in your art, few jump starts are more effective than a week of *reading deprivation*. No reading? That's right: no reading. For most artists, words are like tiny tranquilizers. We have a daily quota of media chat that we swallow up. Like greasy food, it clogs our systems. Too much of it and we feel, yes, fried. Reading deprivation casts us into our inner silence. It is there that we hear the still, small voice. Each of us has an inner dream that we can unfold if we will just have the courage to admit what it is—and the faith to trust our own admission. The admitting is often very difficult. We must have the patience to listen to ourselves carefully.

Creativity—like human life—begins in darkness. We need to acknowledge this. All too often, we think only in terms of light: "And then the lightbulb went on and I got it!" It is true that insights may come to us as flashes. It is true that some of these flashes may be blinding. It is, however, also true that such bright ideas are preceded by a gestation period that is interior, murky, and completely necessary.

We learn by going where we have to go. Exercise is often the going that moves us from stagnation to inspiration, from problem to solution, from self-pity to self-respect. We *do* learn by going. We learn we are stronger than we thought. We learn to look at things with a new perspective. We learn to solve our problems by tapping our own inner resources and listening for inspiration, not only from others but from ourselves. Exercise teaches the rewards of process. It teaches the sense of satisfaction over small tasks well done. Rather than scotch a creative project when it frustrates us, we learn to move through the difficulty. We build spiritual as well as physical stamina.

As an artist, I must be very careful to surround myself with people who nurture my artist—not people who try to overly domesticate it for my own good. Certain friendships will kick off my artistic imagination and others will deaden it.

There is a connection between self-nurturing and self-respect. If I allow myself to be bullied and cowed by other people's urges for me to be more normal or more nice, I sell myself out. They may like me better, feel more comfortable with my more conventional appearance or behavior, but I will hate myself. Hating myself, I may lash out at myself and others. As an artist, my self-respect comes from doing the work. My true friends are those who allow me to work. Creativity is oxygen for our souls. Cutting off our creativity makes us savage. We react like we are being choked. There is a real rage that surfaces when we are interfered with on a level that involves picking lint off of us and fixing us up.

As recovering creatives, many of us find that every time our career heats up we reach for our nearest Wet Blanket. We blurt out our enthusiasm to our most skeptical friend—in fact, we call him up. If we don't, he calls us. This is The Test. In order to achieve escape velocity, we must learn to keep our own counsel, to move silently among doubters, to voice our plans only among our allies, and to name our allies accurately.

Creativity cannot be comfortably quantified in intellectual terms. By its very nature, creativity eschews such containment. In a university where the intellectual life is built upon the art of criticizing—on deconstructing a creative work—the art of creation itself, the art of creative construction, meets with scanty support, understanding, or approval. To be blunt, most academics know how to take something apart, but not how to assemble it. Creativity is a spiritual practice. It is not something that can be perfected, finished, and set aside.

Many academics are themselves artistic beings who are deeply frustrated by their inability to create. Skilled in intellectual discourse, distanced by that intellectual skill from their own creative urgings, they often find the creativity of their charges deeply disturbing. Even the most severe criticism when it fairly hits the mark is apt to be greeted by an internal *ah-hah!* if it shows the artist a new and valid path for work. The criticism that damages is that which disparages, dismisses, ridicules, or condemns. It is frequently vicious but vague and difficult to refute. This is the criticism that damages. As artists we must learn to create our own safe environments. We must learn that when our art reveals a secret of the human soul, those watching it may try to shame us for making it.

As artists, we cannot control all the criticism we will receive. We cannot make our professional critics more healthy or more loving or more constructive than they are. But we can learn to comfort our artist child over unfair criticism; we can learn to find friends with whom we can safely vent our pain. We can learn not to deny and stuff our feelings when we have been artistically savaged.

Much true criticism liberates the artist it is aimed at. We are childlike, not childish. *Ah-hah!* is often the accompanying inner sound when a well-placed, accurate critical arrow makes its mark. The artist thinks, "Yes! I can see that! That's right! I can change that!" The criticism that damages an artist is the criticism—well intentioned or ill—that contains no saving kernel of truth yet has a certain damning plausibility or an unassailable blanket judgment that cannot be rationally refuted. Success occurs in clusters. As artists, we must find those who believe in us, and in whom we believe, and band together for support, encouragement, and protection.

When faced with a loss, immediately take one small action to support your artist. Even if all you are doing is buying a bunch of tulips and a sketch pad, your action says, "I acknowledge you and your pain. I promise you a future worth having." Like a small child, our artist needs mommying. "Ouch. That hurt. Here's a little treat, a lullaby, a promise . . ."

As artists, we belong to an ancient and holy tribe. We are the carriers of the truth that spirit moves through us all. When we deal with one another, we are dealing not merely with our human personalities but also with the unseen but ever-present throng of ideas, visions, stories, poems, songs, sculptures, art-as-facts that crowd the temple of consciousness waiting to be born.

As artists, we are spiritual sharks. The ruthless truth is that if we don't keep moving, we sink to the bottom and die. The choice is very simple: we can insist on resting on our laurels, or we can begin anew. The stringent requirement of a sustained creative life is the humility to start again, to begin anew.

As artists we cannot afford to think about who is getting ahead of us and how they don't deserve it. The desire to *be better than* can choke off the simple desire to be. As artists we cannot afford this thinking. It leads us away from our own voices and choices and into a defensive game that centers outside of ourselves and our sphere of influence. It asks us to define our own creativity in terms of someone else's.

Competition is a spiritual drug. When we focus on competition we poison our own well, impede our own progress. When we are ogling the accomplishments of others, we take our eyes away from our own through line. We ask ourselves the wrong questions, and those wrong questions give us wrong answers. "Am I famous yet?" we ask. Fame is a spiritual drug. It is often a by-product of our artistic work but, like nuclear waste, it can be a very dangerous by-product. Fame, the desire to attain it, the desire to hold on to it, can produce the "How am I doing?" syndrome. This question is not "Is the work going well?" This question is "How does it look to them?" Judging your artistic efforts by these standards is artist abuse.

Jealousy is a map. Each of our jealousy maps differs. Jealousy is always a mask for fear: fear that we aren't able to get what we want; frustration that somebody else seems to be getting what is rightfully ours even if we are too frightened to reach for it. The truth, revealed by action in the direction of our dreams, is that there is room for all of us. But jealousy produces tunnel vision. It narrows our ability to see things in perspective. It strips us of our ability to see other options. The biggest lie that jealousy tells us is that we have no choice but to be jealous. Perversely, jealousy strips us of our will to act when action holds the key to our freedom. Even the biggest changes begin with the small ones. Green is the color of jealousy, but it is also the color of hope. When you learn to harness its fierce energy on your own behalf, jealousy is part of the fuel toward a greener and more verdant future.

When we think about creativity, it is all too easy to think *art* with a capital A. For our purposes, capital-A art is a scarlet letter, branding us as doomed. In order to nurture our creativity, we require a sense of festivity, even humor: "Art. That's somebody my sister used to date." It is a paradox of creative recovery that we must get serious about taking ourselves lightly. We must work at learning to play. Creativity must be freed from the narrow parameters of capital-A art and recognized as having much broader play (that word again).

Only recently recognized as an addiction, workaholism still receives a great deal of support in our society. The phrase "I'm working" has a certain unassailable air of goodness and duty to it. The truth is, we are very often working to avoid ourselves, our spouses, our real feelings. In creative recovery, it is far easier to get people to do the extra work of the Morning Pages than it is to get them to do the assigned play of an artist date. Play can make a workaholic very nervous. Fun is scary.

Many blocked creatives tell themselves they are both too old and too young to allow themselves to pursue their dreams. Old and dotty, they might try it. Young and foolish, they might try it. In either scenario, being crazy is a prerequisite to creative exploration. Creativity occurs in the moment, and in the moment we are timeless. We discover that as we engage in a creative recovery. "I felt like a kid," we may say after a satisfying artist date. Kids are not self-conscious and once we are actually in the flow of our creativity, neither are we.

A believing mirror is a friend to your creativity—someone who believes in you and your creativity. As artists, we can consciously build Creative Clusters—a Sacred Circle of Believing Mirrors to potentiate each other's growth, to mirror a "yes" to each other's creativity. The Sacred Circle is built on respect and trust. The image is of the garden. Each plant has its name and its place. There is no one flower that cancels the need for another. Each bloom has its unique and irreplaceable beauty. *Above All:* God is the source. No human power can deflect our good or create it. We are all conduits for a higher self that would work through us. We are all equally connected to a spiritual source. We do not always know which among us will teach us best. We are all meant to cherish and serve one another. *The Artist's Way* is tribal.

CREATIVE AFFIRMATIONS

1. I am a channel for God's creativity, and my work comes to good.
2. My dreams come from God and God has the power to accomplish them.
3. As I create and listen, I will be led.
4. Creativity is the Creator's will for me.
5. My creativity heals myself and others.
6. I am allowed to nurture my artist.
7. Through the use of a few simple tools, my creativity will flourish.
8. Through the use of my creativity, I serve God.
9. My creativity always leads me to truth and love.
10. My creativity leads me to forgiveness and self-forgiveness.
11. There is a divine plan of goodness for me.
12. There is a divine plan of goodness for my work.

13. As I listen to the creator within, I am led.
14. As I listen to my creativity, I am led to my creator.
15. I am willing to create.
16. I am willing to learn to let myself create.
17. I am willing to let God create through me.
18. I am willing to be of service through my creativity.
19. I am willing to experience my creative energy.
20. I am willing to use my creative talents.

ABOUT THE AUTHOR

JULIA CAMERON, the author of *The Artist's Way*, *The Vein of Gold*, *The Right to Write*, and *God Is No Laughing Matter*, is an active artist who teaches internationally. A poet, playwright, novelist, and composer, she has extensive credits in film, television, and theater.